higher-level thinking Questions
Primary Literature

questions by
Laurie Kagan

created and designed by
Miguel Kagan

illustrated by
Celso Rodriguez

D1227826

Kagan Publishing
981 Calle Amanecer
San Clemente, CA 92673
(949) 545-6300
Fax: (949) 545-6301
1 (800) 933-2667
www.KaganOnline.com

ISBN: 978-1-879097-48-3

Table of Contents

"I had six
honest serving men
They taught me all I knew:
Their names were Where
and What and When
and Why and How and
Who.

— Rudyard Kipling

Higher-Level Thinking Questions for Primary Literature
Kagan Publishing • 1 (800) 933-2667 • www.KaganOnline.com

Introduction

In your hands you hold a powerful book. It is a member of a series of transformative blackline activity books. Between the covers, you will find questions, questions, and more questions! But these are no ordinary questions. These are the important kind—higher-level thinking questions—the kind that stretch your students' minds; the kind that release your students' natural curiosity about the world; the kind that rack your students' brains; the kind that instill in your students a sense of wonderment about your curriculum.

But we are getting a bit ahead of ourselves. Let's start from the beginning. Since this is a book of questions, it seems only appropriate for this introduction to pose a few questions—about the book and its underlying educational philosophy. So Mr. Kipling's Six Honest Serving Men, if you will, please lead the way:

What?
What are higher-level thinking questions?

This is a loaded question (as should be all good questions). Using our analytic thinking skills, let's break this question down into two smaller questions: 1) What is higher-level thinking? and 2) What are questions? When we understand the types of thinking skills and the types of questions, we can combine the best of both worlds, crafting beautiful questions to generate the range of higher-level thinking in our students!

Types of Thinking

There are many different types of thinking. Some types of thinking include:

- applying
- associating
- comparing
- contrasting
- defining
- elaborating
- empathizing
- experimenting
- generalizing
- investigating
- making analogies
- planning
- prioritizing
- recalling
- reflecting
- reversing
- sequencing
- summarizing
- synthesizing
- assessing
- augmenting
- connecting
- decision-making
- drawing conclusions
- eliminating
- evaluating
- explaining
- inferring consequences
- inventing
- memorizing
- predicting
- problem-solving
- reducing
- relating
- role-taking
- substituting
- symbolizing
- understanding
- thinking about thinking (metacognition)

This is quite a formidable list. It's nowhere near complete. Thinking is a big, multifaceted phenomenon. Perhaps the most widely recognized system for classifying thinking and classroom questions is Benjamin Bloom's Taxonomy of Thinking Skills. Bloom's Taxonomy classifies thinking skills into six hierarchical levels. It begins with the lower levels of thinking skills and moves up to higher-level thinking skills: 1) Knowledge, 2) Comprehension, 3) Application, 4) Analysis, 5) Synthesis, 6) Evaluation. See Bloom's Taxonomy on the following page.

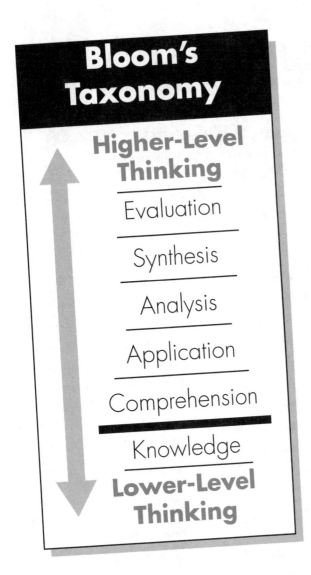

Bloom's Taxonomy

Higher-Level Thinking

Evaluation

Synthesis

Analysis

Application

Comprehension

Knowledge

Lower-Level Thinking

In education, the term "higher-level thinking" often refers to the higher levels of Mr. Bloom's taxonomy. But Bloom's Taxonomy is but one way of organizing and conceptualizing the various types of thinking skills.

There are many ways we can cut the thinking skills pie. We can alternatively view the many different types of thinking skills as, well…many different skills. Some thinking skills may be hierarchical. Some may be interrelated. And some may be relatively independent.

In this book, we take a pragmatic, functional approach. Each type of thinking skill serves a different function. So called "lower-level" thinking skills are very useful for certain purposes. Memorizing and understanding information are

invaluable skills that our students will use throughout their lives. But so too are many of the "higher-level" thinking skills on our list. The more facets of students' thinking skills we develop, the better we prepare them for lifelong success.

Because so much classroom learning heretofore has focused on the "lower rungs" of the thinking skills ladder—knowledge and comprehension, or memorization and understanding—in this series of books we have chosen to focus on questions to generate "higher-level" thinking. This book is an attempt to correct the imbalance in the types of thinking skills developed by classroom questions.

Types of Questions
As we ask questions of our students, we further promote cognitive development when we use Fat questions, Low-Consensus questions, and True questions.

Fat Questions vs. Skinny Questions
Skinny questions are questions that require a skinny answer. For example, after reading a poem, we can ask: "Did you like the poem?" Even though this question could be categorized as an Evaluation question—Bloom's highest level of thinking— it can be answered with one monosyllabic word: "Yes" or "No." How much thinking are we actually generating in our students?

We can reframe this question to make it a fat question: "What things did you like about the poem? What things did you dislike?" Notice no short answer will do. Answering this fattened-up question requires more elaboration. These fat questions presuppose not that there is only one thing but things plural that the student liked and things that she did not like. Making things plural is one way to make skinny questions fat. Students stretch their minds to come up with multiple ideas or solutions. Other easy ways to

Higher-Level Thinking Questions for Primary Literature
Kagan Publishing • 1 (800) 933-2667 • www.KaganOnline.com

make questions fat is to add "Why or why not?" or "Explain" or "Describe" or "Defend your position" to the end of a question. These additions promote elaboration beyond a skinny answer. Because language and thought are intimately intertwined, questions that require elaborate responses stretch students' thinking: They grapple to articulate their thoughts.

The type of questions we ask impact not just the type of thinking we develop in our students, but also the depth of thought. Fat questions elicit fat responses. Fat responses develop both depth of thinking and range of thinking skills. The questions in this book are designed to elicit fat responses—deep and varied thinking.

High-Consensus Questions vs. Low-Consensus Questions

A high-consensus question is one to which most people would give the same response, usually a right or wrong answer. After learning about sound, we can ask our students: "What is the name of a room specially designed to improve acoustics for the audience?" This is a high-consensus question. The answer (auditorium) is either correct or incorrect.

Compare the previous question with a low-consensus question: "If you were going to build an auditorium, what special design features would you take into consideration?" Notice, to the low-consensus question there is no right or wrong answer. Each person formulates his or her unique response. To answer, students must apply what they learned, use their ingenuity and creativity.

High-consensus questions promote convergent thinking. With high-consensus questions we strive to direct students *what to think*. Low-consensus questions promote divergent thinking, both critical and creative. With low-consen-

sus questions we strive to develop students' *ability to think*. The questions in this book are low-consensus questions designed to promote independent, critical and creative thought.

True Questions vs. Review Questions

We all know what review questions are. They're the ones in the back of every chapter and unit. Review questions ask students to regurgitate previously stated or learned information. For example, after learning about the rain forest we may ask: "What percent of the world's oxygen does the rain forest produce?" Students can go back a few pages in their books or into their memory banks and pull out the answer. This is great if we are working on memorization skills, but does little to develop "higher-order" thinking skills.

True questions, on the other hand, are meaningful questions—questions to which we do not know the answer. For example: "What might happen if all the world's rain forests were cut down?" This is a hypothetical; we don't know the answer but considering the question forces us to think. We infer some logical consequences based on what we know. The goal of true questions is not a correct answer, but the thinking journey students take to create a meaningful response. True questions are more representative of real life. Seldom is there a black and white answer. In life, we struggle with ambiguity, confounding variables, and uncertain outcomes. There are millions of shades of gray. True questions prepare students to deal with life's uncertainties.

When we ask a review question, we know the answer and are checking to see if the student does also. When we ask a true question, it is truly a question. We don't necessarily know the answer and neither does the student. True

> **Education is not the filling of a pail, but the lighting of a fire.**
> — William Butler Yeats

Types of Questions

Skinny ➡ **Fat**
- Short Answer
- Shallow Thinking
- Elaborated Answer
- Deep Thinking

High-Consensus ➡ **Low-Consensus**
- Right or Wrong Answer
- Develops Convergent Thinking
- "What" to Think
- No Single Correct Answer
- Develops Divergent Thinking
- "How" to Think

Review ➡ **True**
- Asker Knows Answer
- Checking for Correctness
- Asker Doesn't Know Answer
- Invitation to Think

questions are often an invitation to think, ponder, speculate, and engage in a questioning process.

We can use true questions in the classroom to make our curriculum more personally meaningful, to promote investigation, and awaken students' sense of awe and wonderment in what we teach. Many questions you will find in this book are true questions designed to make the content provocative, intriguing, and personally relevant.

The box above summarizes the different types of questions. The questions you will find in this book are a move away from skinny, high-consensus, review questions toward fat, low-consensus true questions. As we ask these types of questions in our class, we transform even mundane content into a springboard for higher-level thinking. As we integrate these question gems into our daily lessons, we create powerful learning experiences. *We do not fill our students' pails with knowledge; we kindle their fires to become lifetime thinkers.*

 **Why?**
Why should I use higher-level thinking questions in my classroom?

As we enter the new millennium, major shifts in our economic structure are changing the ways we work and live. The direction is increasingly toward an information-based, high-tech economy. The sum of our technological information is exploding. We could give you a figure how rapidly information is doubling, but by the time you read this, the number would be outdated! No kidding.

But this is no surprise. This is our daily reality. We see it around us everyday and on the news: cloning, gene manipulation, e-mail, the Internet, Mars rovers, electric cars, hybrids, laser surgery, CD-ROMs, DVDs. All around us we see the wheels of progress turning: New discoveries, new technologies, a new societal knowledge and information base. New jobs are being created

Higher-Level Thinking Questions for Primary Literature
Kagan Publishing • 1 (800) 933-2667 • www.KaganOnline.com

today in fields that simply didn't exist yesterday.

How do we best prepare our students for this uncertain future—a future in which the only constant will be change? As we are propelled into a world of ever-increasing change, what is the relative value of teaching students facts versus thinking skills? This point becomes even more salient when we realize that students cannot master everything, and many facts will soon become obsolete. Facts become outdated or irrelevant. Thinking skills are for a lifetime. Increasingly, how we define educational success will be away from the quantity of information mastered. Instead, we will define success as our students' ability to generate questions, apply, synthesize, predict, evaluate, compare, categorize.

If we as a professionals are to proactively respond to these societal shifts, thinking skills will become central to our curriculum. Whether we teach thinking skills directly, or we integrate them into our curriculum, the power to think is the greatest gift we can give our students!

We believe the questions you will find in this book are a step in the direction of preparing students for lifelong success. The goal is to develop independent thinkers who are critical and creative, regardless of the content. We hope the books in this series are more than sets of questions. We provide them as a model approach to questioning in the classroom.

On pages 8 and 9, you will find Questions to Engage Students' Thinking Skills. These pages contain numerous types of thinking and questions designed to engage each thinking skill. As you make your own questions for your students with your own content, use these question starters to help you frame your

> ## Virtually the only predictable trend is continuing change.
> — Dr. Linda Tsantis,
> Creating the Future

questions to stimulate various facets of your students' thinking skills. Also let your students use these question starters to generate their own higher-level thinking questions about the curriculum.

Who?
Who is this book for?

This book is for you and your students, but mostly for your students. It is designed to help make your job easier. Inside you will find hundreds of ready-to-use reproducible questions. Sometimes in the press for time we opt for what is easy over what is best. These books attempt to make easy what is best. In this treasure chest, you will find hours and hours of timesaving ready-made questions and activities.

Place Higher-Level Thinking In Your Students' Hands

As previously mentioned, this book is even more for your students than for you. As teachers, we ask a tremendous number of questions. Primary teachers ask 3.5 to 6.5 questions per minute! Elementary teachers average 348 questions a day. How many questions would you predict our students ask? Researchers asked this question. What they found was shocking: Typical students ask approximately one question per month.* One question per month!

Although this study may not be representative of your classroom, it does suggest that in general, as teachers we are missing out on a very powerful force—student-generated questions. The capacity to answer higher-level thinking questions is a

---

* Myra & David Sadker, "Questioning Skills" in *Classroom Teaching Skills*, 2nd ed. Lexington, MA: D.C. Heath & Co., 1982.

Questions to Engage Students' Thinking Skills

Analyzing
• How could you break down…?
• What components…?
• What qualities/characteristics…?

Applying
• How is _____ an example of…?
• What practical applications…?
• What examples…?
• How could you use…?
• How does this apply to…?
• In your life, how would you apply…?

Assessing
• By what criteria would you assess…?
• What grade would you give…?
• How could you improve…?

Augmenting/Elaborating
• What ideas might you add to…?
• What more can you say about…?

Categorizing/Classifying/Organizing
• How might you classify…?
• If you were going to categorize…?

Comparing/Contrasting
• How would you compare…?
• What similarities…?
• What are the differences between…?
• How is _____ different…?

Connecting/Associating
• What do you already know about…?
• What connections can you make between…?
• What things do you think of when you think of…?

Decision-Making
• How would you decide…?
• If you had to choose between…?

Defining
• How would you define…?
• In your own words, what is…?

Describing/Summarizing
• How could you describe/summarize…?
• If you were a reporter, how would you describe…?

Determining Cause/Effect
• What is the cause of…?
• How does _____ effect _____?
• What impact might…?

Drawing Conclusions/ Inferring Consequences
• What conclusions can you draw from…?
• What would happen if…?
• What would have happened if…?
• If you changed _____, what might happen?

Eliminating
• What part of _____ might you eliminate?
• How could you get rid of…?

Evaluating
• What is your opinion about…?
• Do you prefer…?
• Would you rather…?
• What is your favorite…?
• Do you agree or disagree…?
• What are the positive and negative aspects of…?
• What are the advantages and disadvantages…?
• If you were a judge…?
• On a scale of 1 to 10, how would you rate…?
• What is the most important…?
• Is it better or worse…?

Explaining
• How can you explain…?
• What factors might explain…?

Higher-Level Thinking Questions for Primary Literature
Kagan Publishing • 1 (800) 933-2667 • www.KaganOnline.com

Experimenting
- How could you test...?
- What experiment could you do to...?

Generalizing
- What general rule can...?
- What principle could you apply...?
- What can you say about all...?

Interpreting
- Why is _____ important?
- What is the significance of...?
- What role...?
- What is the moral of...?

Inventing
- What could you invent to...?
- What machine could...?

Investigating
- How could you find out more about...?
- If you wanted to know about...?

Making Analogies
- How is _____ like _____?
- What analogy can you invent for...?

Observing
- What observations did you make about...?
- What changes...?

Patterning
- What patterns can you find...?
- How would you describe the organization of...?

Planning
- What preparations would you...?

Predicting/Hypothesizing
- What would you predict...?
- What is your theory about...?
- If you were going to guess...?

Prioritizing
- What is more important...?
- How might you prioritize...?

Problem-Solving
- How would you approach the problem?
- What are some possible solutions to...?

Reducing/Simplifying
- In a word, how would you describe...?
- How can you simplify...?

Reflecting/Metacognition
- What would you think if...?
- How can you describe what you were thinking when...?

Relating
- How is _____ related to _____?
- What is the relationship between...?
- How does _____ depend on _____?

Reversing/Inversing
- What is the opposite of...?

Role-Taking/Empathizing
- If you were (someone/something else)...?
- How would you feel if...?

Sequencing
- How could you sequence...?
- What steps are involved in...?

Substituting
- What could have been used instead of...?
- What else could you use for...?
- What might you substitute for...?
- What is another way...?

Symbolizing
- How could you draw...?
- What symbol best represents...?

Synthesizing
- How could you combine...?
- What could you put together...?

wonderful skill we can give our students, as is the skill to solve problems. Arguably more important skills are the ability to find problems to solve and formulate questions to answer. If we look at the great thinkers of the world—the Einsteins, the Edisons, the Freuds—their thinking is marked by a yearning to solve tremendous questions and problems. It is this questioning process that distinguishes those who illuminate and create our world from those who merely accept it.

Make Learning an Interactive Process

Higher-level thinking is not just something that occurs between students' ears! Students benefit from an interactive process. This basic premise underlies the majority of activities you will find in this book.

As students discuss questions and listen to others, they are confronted with differing perspectives and are pushed to articulate their own thinking well beyond the level they could attain on their own. Students too have an enormous capacity to mediate each other's learning. When we heterogeneously group students to work together, we create an environment to move students through their zone of proximal development. We also provide opportunities for tutoring and leadership. Verbal interaction with peers in cooperative groups adds a dimension to questions not available with whole-class questions and answers.

> **Asking a good question requires students to think harder than giving a good answer.**
> — Robert Fisher, Teaching Children to Learn

Reflect on this analogy: If we wanted to teach our students to catch and throw, we could bring in one tennis ball and take turns throwing it to each student and having them throw it back to us. Alternatively, we could bring in twenty balls and have our students form small groups and have them toss the ball back and forth to each other. Picture the two classrooms: One with twenty balls being caught at any one moment, and the other with just one. In which class would students better and more quickly learn to catch and throw?

The same is true with thinking skills. When we make our students more active participants in the learning process, they are given dramatically more opportunities to produce their own thought and to strengthen their own thinking skills. Would you rather have one question being asked and answered at any one moment in your class, or twenty? Small groups mean more questioning and more thinking. Instead of rarely answering a teacher question or rarely generating their own question, asking and answering questions becomes a regular part of your students' day. It is through cooperative interaction that we truly turn our classroom into a higher-level think tank. The associated personal and social benefits are invaluable.

When?
When do I use higher-level thinking questions?

Do I use these questions at the beginning of the lesson, during the lesson, or after? The answer, of course, is all of the above.

Use these questions or your own thinking questions at the beginning of the lesson to provide a motivational set for the lesson. Pique students' interest about the content with some provocative questions: "What would happen if we didn't have gravity?" "Why did Pilgrims get along with some Native Americans, but not others?" "What do you think this book will be about?" Make the content personally relevant by bringing in students' own knowledge, experiences, and feelings about the content: "What do you know about spiders?" "What things do you like about mystery stories?" "How would you feel if explorers invaded your land and killed your family?" "What do you wonder about electricity?"

Use the higher-level thinking questions throughout your lessons. Use the many questions and activities in this book not as a replacement of your curriculum, but as an additional avenue to explore the content and stretch students' thinking skills.

Use the questions after your lesson. Use the higher-level thinking questions, a journal writing activity, or the question starters as an extension activity to your lesson or unit.

Or just use the questions as stand-alone sponge activities for students or teams who have finished their work and need a challenging project to work on.

It doesn't matter when you use them, just use them frequently. As questioning becomes a habitual part of the classroom day, students' fear of asking silly questions is diminished. As the ancient Chinese proverb states, "Those who ask a silly question may seem a fool for five minutes, but those who do not ask remain a fool for life."

The important thing is to never stop questioning.
— Albert Einstein

As teachers, we should make a conscious effort to ensure that a portion of the many questions we ask on a daily basis are those that move our students beyond rote memorization. When we integrate higher-level thinking questions into our daily lessons, we transform our role from transmitters of knowledge to engineers of learning.

Where?
Where should I keep this book?

Keep it close by. Inside there are 16 sets of questions. Pull it out any time you teach these topics or need a quick, easy, fun activity or journal writing topic.

How?
How do I get the most out of this book?

In this book you will find 16 topics arranged alphabetically. For each topic there are reproducible pages for: 1) 16 Question Cards, 2) a Journal Writing activity page, 3) and a Question Starters activity page.

1. Question Cards

The Question Cards are truly the heart of this book. There are numerous ways the Question Cards can be used. After the other activity pages are introduced, you will find a description of a variety of engaging formats to use the Question Cards.

Specific and General Questions

Some of the questions provided in this book series are content-specific and others are content-free. For example, the literature questions in the Literature books are content-specific. Questions for the Great Kapok Tree deal specifically with that literature selection. Some language arts questions in the Language Arts book, on the other hand, are content-free. They are general questions that can be used over and over again with new content. For example, the Book Review questions can be used after reading any book. The Story Structure questions can be used after reading any story. You can tell by glancing at the title of the set and some of the questions whether the set is content-specific or content-free.

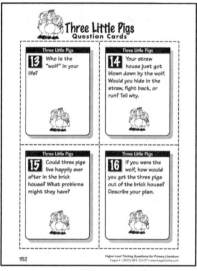

A Little Disclaimer

Not all of the "questions" on the Question Cards are actually questions. Some instruct students to do something. For example, "Compare and contrast..." We can also use these directives to develop the various facets of students' thinking skills.

The Power of Think Time

As you and your students use these questions, don't forget about the power of Think Time! There are two different think times. The first is the time between the question and the response. The second is the time between the response and feedback on the response. Think time has been shown to greatly enhance the quality of student thinking. If students are not pausing for either think time, or doing it too briefly, emphasize its importance. Five little seconds of silent think time after the question and five more seconds before feedback are proven, powerful ways to promote higher-level thinking in your class.

Use Your Question Cards for Years

For attractive Question Cards that will last for years, photocopy them on color card-stock paper and laminate them. To save time, have the Materials Monitor from each team pick up one card set, a pair of scissors for the team, and an envelope or rubber band. Each team cuts out their own set of Question Cards. When they are done with the activity, students can place the Question Cards in the envelope and write the name of the set on the envelope or wrap the cards with a rubber band for storage.

2. Journal Question

The Journal Writing page contains one of the 16 questions as a journal writing prompt. You can substitute any question, or use one of your own. The power of journal writing cannot be overstated. The act of writing takes longer than speaking and thinking. It allows the brain time to make deep connections to the content. Writing requires the writer to present his or her response in a clear, concise language. Writing develops both strong thinking and communication skills.

A helpful activity before journal writing is to have students discuss the question in pairs or in small teams. Students discuss their ideas and what they plan to write. This little prewriting activity ignites ideas for those students who stare blankly at their Journal Writing page. The interpersonal interaction further helps students articulate what they are thinking about the topic and invites students to delve deeper into the topic.

Tell students before they write that they will share their journal entries with a partner or with their team. This motivates many students to improve their entry. Sharing written responses also promotes flexible thinking with open-ended questions, and allows students to hear their peers' responses, ideas and writing styles.

Have students keep a collection of their journal entries in a three-ring binder. This way you can collect them if you wish for assessment or have students go back to reflect on their own learning. If you are using questions across the curriculum, each subject can have its own journal or own section within the binder. Use the provided blackline on the following page for a cover for students' journals or have students design their own.

3. Question Starters

The Question Starters activity page is designed to put the questions in the hands of your students. Use these question starters to scaffold your students' ability to write their own thinking questions. This page includes eight question starters to direct students to generate questions across the levels and types of thinking. This Question Starters activity page can be used in a few different ways:

Individual Questions

Have students independently come up with their own questions. When done, they can trade their questions with a partner. On a separate sheet of paper students answer their partners' questions. After answering, partners can share how they answered each other's questions.

JOURNAL

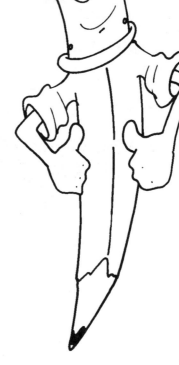

My Best Thinking

_____

This Journal Belongs to

Higher-Level Thinking Questions for Primary Literature
Kagan Publishing • 1 (800) 933-2667 • www.KaganOnline.com

Pair Questions

Students work in pairs to generate questions to send to another pair. Partners take turns writing each question and also take turns recording each answer. After answering, pairs pair up to share how they answered each other's questions.

Team Questions

Students work in teams to generate questions to send to another team. Teammates take turns writing each question and recording each answer. After answering, teams pair up to share how they answered each other's questions.

Teacher-Led Questions

For young students, lead the whole class in coming up with good higher-level thinking questions.

Teach Your Students About Thinking and Questions

An effective tool to improve students' thinking skills is to teach students about the types of thinking skills and types of questions. Teaching students about the types of thinking skills improves their metacognitive abilities. When students are aware of the types of thinking, they may more effectively plan, monitor, and evaluate their own thinking. When students understand the types of questions and the basics of question construction, they are more likely to create effective higher-level thinking questions. In doing so they develop their own thinking skills and the thinking of classmates as they work to answer each other's questions.

Table of Activities

The Question Cards can be used in a variety of game-like formats to forge students' thinking skills. They can be used for cooperative team and pair work, for whole-class questioning, for independent activities, or at learning centers. On the following pages you will find numerous excellent options to use your Question Cards. As you use the Question Cards in this book, try the different activities listed below to add novelty and variety to the higher-level thinking process.

Higher-Level Thinking Question Card
Activities

team activity #1

Question Commander

Preferably in teams of four, students shuffle their Question Cards and place them in a stack, questions facing down, so that all teammates can easily reach the Question Cards. Give each team a Question Commander set of instructions (blackline provided on following page) to lead them through each question.

Student One becomes the Question Commander for the first question. The Question Commander reads the question aloud to the team, then asks the teammates to think about the question and how they would answer it. After the think time, the Question Commander selects a teammate to answer the question. The Question Commander can spin a spinner or roll a die to select who will answer. After the teammate gives the answer, Question Commander again calls for think time, this time asking the team to think about the answer. After the think time, the Question Commander leads a team discus-

sion in which any teammember can contribute his or her thoughts or ideas to the question, or give praise or reactions to the answer.

When the discussion is over, Student Two becomes the Question Commander for the next question.

Higher-Level Thinking Questions for Primary Literature
Kagan Publishing • 1 (800) 933-2667 • www.KaganOnline.com

Question Commander
Instruction Cards

Question Commander

1. Ask the Question:
Question Commander reads the question to the team.
2. Think Time: "Think of your best answer."
3. Answer the Question:
The Question Commander selects a teammate to answer the question.
4. Think Time: "Think about how you would answer differently or add to the answer."
5. Team Discussion: As a team, discuss other possible answers or reactions to the answer given.

Question Commander

1. Ask the Question:
Question Commander reads the question to the team.
2. Think Time: "Think of your best answer."
3. Answer the Question:
The Question Commander selects a teammate to answer the question.
4. Think Time: "Think about how you would answer differently or add to the answer."
5. Team Discussion: As a team, discuss other possible answers or reactions to the answer given.

Question Commander

1. Ask the Question:
Question Commander reads the question to the team.
2. Think Time: "Think of your best answer."
3. Answer the Question:
The Question Commander selects a teammate to answer the question.
4. Think Time: "Think about how you would answer differently or add to the answer."
5. Team Discussion: As a team, discuss other possible answers or reactions to the answer given.

Question Commander

1. Ask the Question:
Question Commander reads the question to the team.
2. Think Time: "Think of your best answer."
3. Answer the Question:
The Question Commander selects a teammate to answer the question.
4. Think Time: "Think about how you would answer differently or add to the answer."
5. Team Discussion: As a team, discuss other possible answers or reactions to the answer given.

Fan-N-Pick

In a team of four, Student One fans out the question cards, and says, "Pick a card, any card!" Student Two picks a card and reads the question out loud to teammates. After five seconds of think time, Student Three gives his or her answer. After another five seconds of think time, Student Four paraphrases, praises, or adds to the answer given. Students rotate roles for each new round.

Spin-N-Think

Spin-N-Think spinners are available from Kagan to lead teams through the steps of higher-level thinking. Students spin the Spin-N-Think™ spinner to select a student at each stage of the questioning to: 1) ask the question, 2) answer the question, 3) paraphrase and praise the answer, 4) augment the answer, and 5) discuss the question or answer. The Spin-N-Think™ game makes higher-level thinking more fun, and holds students accountable because they are often called upon, but never know when their number will come up.

Three-Step Interview

After the question is read to the team, students pair up. The first step is an interview in which one student interviews the other about the question. In the second step, students remain with their partner but switch roles: The interviewer becomes the interviewee. In the third step, the pairs come back together and each student in turn presents to the team what their partner shared. Three-Step Interview is strong for individual accountability, active listening, and paraphrasing skills.

Team Discussion

Team Discussion is an easy and informal way of processing the questions: Students read a question and then throw it open for discussion. Team Discussion, however, does not ensure that there is individual accountability or equal participation.

Think-Pair-Square

One student reads a question out loud to teammates. Partners on the same side of the table then pair up to discuss the question and their answers. Then, all four students come together for an open discussion about the question.

Question-Write-RoundRobin

Students take turns asking the team the question. After each question is asked, each student writes his or her ideas on a piece of paper. After students have finished writing, in turn they share their ideas. This format creates strong individual accountability because each student is expected to develop and share an answer for every question.

Mix-Pair-Discuss

Each student gets a different Question Card. For 16 to 32 students, use two sets of questions. In this case, some students may have the same question which is OK. Students get out of their seats and mix around the classroom. They pair up with a partner. One partner reads his or her Question Card and the other answers. Then they switch roles. When done they trade cards and find a new partner. The process is repeated for a predetermined amount of time. The rule is students cannot pair up with the same partner twice. Students may get the same questions twice or more, but each time it is with a new partner. This strategy is a fun, energizing way to ask and answer questions.

Think-Pair-Share

Think-Pair-Share is teacher-directed. The teacher asks the question, then gives students think time. Students then pair up to share their thoughts about the question. After the pair discussion, one student is called on to share with the class what was shared in his or her pair. Think-Pair-Share does not provide as much active participation for students as Think-Pair-Square because only one student is called upon at a time, but is a nice way to do whole-class sharing.

Inside-Outside Circle

Each student gets a Question Card. Half of the students form a circle facing out. The other half forms a circle around the inside circle; each student in the outside circle faces one student in the inside circle. Students in the outside circle ask inside circle students a question. After the inside circle students answer the question, students switch roles questioning and answering. After both have asked and answered a question, they each praise theother's answers and then hold up a hand indicating they are finished. When most students have a hand up, have students trade cards with their partner and rotate to a new partner. To rotate, tell the outside circle to move to the left. This format is a lively and enjoyable way to ask questions and have students listen to the thinking of many classmates.

Question & Answer

This might sound familiar: Instead of giving students the Question Cards, the teacher asks the questions and calls on one student at a time to answer. This traditional format eliminates simultaneous, cooperative interaction, but may be good for introducing younger students to higher-level questions.

Numbered Heads Together

Students number off in their teams so that every student has a number. The teacher asks a question. Students put their "heads together" to discuss the question. The teacher then calls on a number and selects a student with that number to share what his or her team discussed.

pair activity #1

RallyRobin

Each pair gets a set of Question Cards. Student A in the pair reads the question out loud to his or her partner. Student B answers. Partners take turns asking and answering each question.

Pair Discussion

Partners take turns asking the question. The pair then discusses the answer together. Unlike RallyRobin, students discuss the answer. Both students contribute to answering and to discussing each other's ideas.

Question-Write-Share-Discuss

One partner reads the Question Card out loud to his or her teammate. Both students write down their ideas. Partners take turns sharing what they wrote. Partners discuss how their ideas are similar and different.

Journal Writing

Students pick one Question Card and make a journal entry or use the question as the prompt for an essay or creative writing. Have students share their writing with a partner or in turn with teammates.

Independent Answers

Students each get their own set of Questions Cards. Pairs or teams can share a set of questions, or the questions can be written on the board or put on the overhead projector. Students work by themselves to answer the questions on a separate sheet of paper. When done, students can compare their answers with a partner, teammates, or the whole class.

Center Ideas

1. Question Card Center

At one center, have the Question Cards and a Spin-N-Think™ spinner, Question Commander instruction card, or Fan-N-Pick instructions. Students lead themselves through the thinking questions. For individual accountability, have each student record their own answer for each question.

2. Journal Writing Center

At a second center, have a Journal Writing activity page for each student. Students can discuss the question with others at their center, then write their own journal entry. After everyone is done writing, students share what they wrote with other students at their center.

3. Question Starters Center

At a third center, have a Question Starters page. Split the students at the center into two groups. Have both groups create thinking questions using the Question Starters activity page. When the groups are done writing their questions, they trade questions with the other group at their center. When done answering each other's questions, two groups pair up to compare their answers.

Alexander and the Terrible, Horrible, No Good, Very Bad Day

higher-level thinking questions

"It is not the answer that enlightens, but the question.

— Eugène Ionesco

Higher-Level Thinking Questions for Primary Literature
Kagan Publishing • 1 (800) 933-2667 • www.KaganOnline.com

Alexander and the Terrible...
Question Cards

Alexander and the Terrible...

1 What might Alexander have done differently to make his day better?

Alexander and the Terrible...

2 When was the last time you had a terrible, horrible, bad day?

Alexander and the Terrible...

3 Why did Alexander keep thinking about Australia? Have you ever thought about leaving when times got tough?

Alexander and the Terrible...

4 Make up another day for Alexander with some good, exciting happenings.

Alexander and the Terrible...
Question Cards

5 Alexander and his brothers ate cereal for breakfast. What did you have for breakfast today? Was it well-balanced? Why or why not?

6 Would you want Alexander for a friend? Explain your answer.

7 Suppose you are Alexander's friend. How would you help him turn his day around?

8 When Alexander said, "If I don't sit by a window, I'll get car sick," no one paid attention. Why not?

Higher-Level Thinking Questions for Primary Literature
Kagan Publishing • 1 (800) 933-2667 • www.KaganOnline.com

Alexander and the Terrible.
Question Cards

Alexander and the Terrible...

9 If Alexander had put away his skateboard and put his chewing gum in the trash can the night before, do you think his day might have started better? What might you do today to make tomorrow a better day?

Alexander and the Terrible...

10 Alexander said things to Paul because he was not his best friend anymore. It made matters worse. Have you ever said something when you were mad, and later were sorry you said it?

Alexander and the Terrible...

11 Name a few things Alexander could have done at lunchtime to turn his day around.

Alexander and the Terrible...

12 Do we make bad days happen, or do they just happen no matter what?

Alexander and the Terrible...
Question Cards

13 Can you think of some other bad things that could have happened to Alexander that day?

14 What could Alexander have done when he did not want the white sneakers?

15 Mrs. Dickens chose Paul's picture of the sailboat instead of Alexander's invisible castle. Why do you think she did that?

16 What are the signs or signals you notice that tell you that you started the day off badly?

Higher-Level Thinking Questions for Primary Literature
Kagan Publishing • 1 (800) 933-2667 • www.KaganOnline.com

Alexander...

Journal Writing Question

Write your response to the question below.
Be ready to share your response.

When was the last time you had a terrible, horrible, bad day? Describe it.

_____

_____

_____

_____

_____

_____

_____

_____

_____

_____

_____

_____

_____

_____

_____

_____

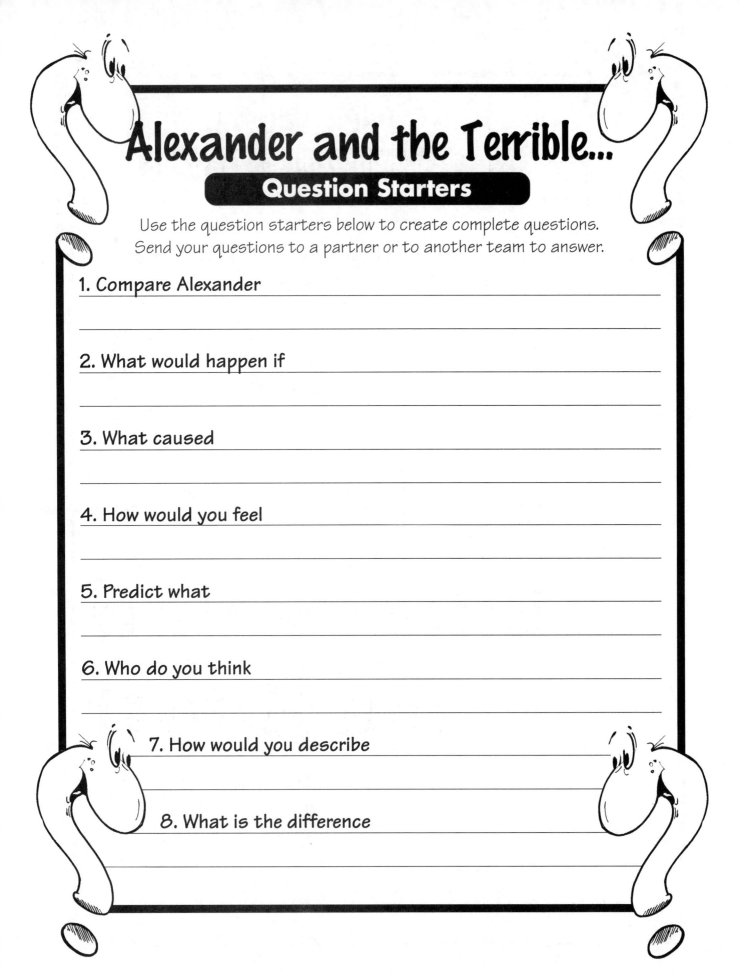

Alexander and the Terrible...

Question Starters

Use the question starters below to create complete questions.
Send your questions to a partner or to another team to answer.

1. Compare Alexander

2. What would happen if

3. What caused

4. How would you feel

5. Predict what

6. Who do you think

7. How would you describe

8. What is the difference

Higher-Level Thinking Questions for Primary Literature
Kagan Publishing • 1 (800) 933-2667 • www.KaganOnline.com

Beauty and the Beast

higher-level thinking questions

The important thing is to never stop questioning.

— Albert Einstein

Higher-Level Thinking Questions for Primary Literature
Kagan Publishing • 1 (800) 933-2667 • www.KaganOnline.com

Beauty and the Beast
Question Cards

Beauty and the Beast

1 How would you have felt if you were Belle and were held captive in the castle?

Beauty and the Beast

2 Why were the townspeople afraid of the Beast? Why wasn't Belle?

Beauty and the Beast

3 What might have happened if the Beast were not turned back into a prince?

Beauty and the Beast

4 Do you think Belle made the right decision in the end? Why or why not?

Beauty and the Beast
Question Cards

Beauty and the Beast

5 What might you have done if you were the one that was turned into a beast?

Beauty and the Beast

6 Describe the relationship between the Beauty and the Beast.

Beauty and the Beast

7 Predict what might happen if the story continued.

Beauty and the Beast

8 Did the prince learn his lesson in the end? How do we know?

Higher-Level Thinking Questions for Primary Literature
Kagan Publishing • 1 (800) 933-2667 • www.KaganOnline.com

Beauty and the Beast

9 How would you treat the Beast if you were Belle?

Beauty and the Beast

10 Which event in the story would you like to have happen to you?

Beauty and the Beast

11 What would you have done if you were Belle?

Beauty and the Beast

12 Was it the right thing for Belle to do when she burst into the castle to save her father?

Beauty and the Beast
Question Cards

Beauty and the Beast

13 How would the story change if the Beast told it? Tell the story from the Beast's point of view.

Beauty and the Beast

14 Think of one word to describe the Beast.

Beauty and the Beast

15 Pretend Belle did not like the Beast. How would the story change?

Beauty and the Beast

16 Name one way the Beast showed himself to be "good" and one way in which he was "bad."

Higher-Level Thinking Questions for Primary Literature
Kagan Publishing • 1 (800) 933-2667 • www.KaganOnline.com

Beauty and the Beast
Journal Writing Question

Write your response to the question below.
Be ready to share your response.

How would the story change if the Beast told it? Tell the story from the Beast's point of view.

_____

_____

_____

_____

_____

_____

_____

_____

_____

_____

_____

_____

_____

_____

_____

_____

_____

_____

_____

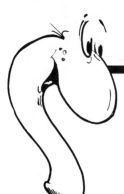

Beauty and the Beast

Question Starters

Use the question starters below to create complete questions.
Send your questions to a partner or to another team to answer.

1. Why do you think the Beast

2. How would you describe

3. What might happen if

4. Where do you think

5. If you were Belle

6. How would you feel if

7. What can you say about

8. In your life

Higher-Level Thinking Questions for Primary Literature
Kagan Publishing • 1 (800) 933-2667 • www.KaganOnline.com

Cinderella

higher-level thinking questions

Teacher: Two kinds: the kind that fill you with so much quail shot that you can't move, and the kind that just give you a little prod behind and you jump to the skies.

— Robert Frost

Cinderella
Question Cards

Cinderella

1 What three things would you like a fairy godmother to do for you?

Cinderella

2 Why did the fairy godmother let Cinderella go to the ball?

Cinderella

3 Would the prince and Cinderella really live happily ever after? Explain what adjustments Cinderella would have to make.

Cinderella

4 What would happen in the story if you were Cinderella and your foot had swollen, and did not fit into the glass slipper?

Cinderella
Question Cards

Cinderella

5 Cinderella did chores around the house. What chores don't you like to do at your house? What would you assign Cinderella to do?

Cinderella

6 How do you think Cinderella felt as she watched her stepsisters try to fit their big feet into the slipper?

Cinderella

7 In the story, the stepmother was an evil character. Suppose the stepmother were a nice, kind person. How would the story change?

Cinderella

8 Name three qualities the Fairy Godmother has that Cinderella's stepmother does not have.

Higher-Level Thinking Questions for Primary Literature
Kagan Publishing • 1 (800) 933-2667 • www.KaganOnline.com

Cinderella
Question Cards

Cinderella

9 What amazed Cinderella the most as she walked into the castle?

Cinderella

10 Pretend you are interviewing Cinderella. What questions would you ask her?

Cinderella

11 Describe the most exciting event that has ever happened to you.

Cinderella

12 How is Cinderella like or unlike you? Explain.

Cinderella
Question Cards

Cinderella

13 Cinderella got her name because one of her chores was "sweeping the cinders." Give Cinderella another name. Explain your choice.

Cinderella

14 The prince sent a footman through the entire village with the glass slipper. Name two other ways the prince could have found Cinderella.

Cinderella

15 What might have happened to the stepsisters after the prince and Cinderella got married? Where and how would they live?

Cinderella

16 Pretend you had the fairy godmother's magic wand. On what adventure would you send yourself?

Higher-Level Thinking Questions for Primary Literature
Kagan Publishing • 1 (800) 933-2667 • www.KaganOnline.com

Cinderella
Journal Writing Question

Write your response to the question below.
Be ready to share your response.

Pretend you had the fairy godmother's magic wand. On what adventure would you send yourself?

_____
_____
_____
_____
_____
_____
_____
_____
_____
_____
_____
_____
_____
_____
_____
_____
_____
_____
_____
_____
_____

Cinderella

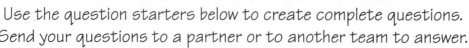

Question Starters

Use the question starters below to create complete questions.
Send your questions to a partner or to another team to answer.

1. Why is the Cinderella's stepmother _____

_____

2. What role did _____

_____

3. How did you feel _____

_____

4. What is your favorite _____

_____

5. What would have happened if _____

_____

6. How would you compare _____

_____

7. Why if the prince _____

8. If you were Cinderella _____

_____

Higher-Level Thinking Questions for Primary Literature
Kagan Publishing • 1 (800) 933-2667 • www.KaganOnline.com

Frog and Toad Are Friends

higher-level thinking questions

"Teach the young people how to think, not what to think.

— Sidney Sugarman "

Frog and Toad Are Friends
Question Cards

Frog and Toad Are Friends

1 What are some of the qualities of a good friendship?

Frog and Toad Are Friends

2 Frog and Toad are different, but they still have a good friendship. How is this possible?

Frog and Toad Are Friends

3 You have just become the author and you are writing a new chapter for the book. Describe a new adventure for Frog and Toad.

Frog and Toad Are Friends

4 If Frog kissed a princess and turned into a handsome prince, what might happen to Toad?

Frog and Toad Are Friends
Question Cards

5 Are Frog and Toad brave? List the reasons for your answer.

6 Which of Frog and Toad's adventures do you think is the most dangerous? Did they react well?

7 If you became one character, who would you choose — Frog or Toad? Why?

8 What part of the book did you enjoy most? Why?

Higher-Level Thinking Questions for Primary Literature
Kagan Publishing • 1 (800) 933-2667 • www.KaganOnline.com

Frog and Toad Are Friends
Question Cards

Frog and Toad Are Friends

9 What other stories have you read that are similar to this one? Explain why.

Frog and Toad Are Friends

10 Do you have a good friend? What do you value about that friendship?

Frog and Toad Are Friends

11 How might the story change if it were about a crocodile and alligator instead of a frog and toad?

Frog and Toad Are Friends

12 Were the main characters more like humans than animals? Explain.

Frog and Toad Are Friends
Question Cards

13 Would you like to jump into the pages and have an adventure with Frog and Toad? What kind of animal would you be and what role would you take?

14 You are now a trio, "Frog, Toad, and You." On what new adventure would you like to take your two best friends?

15 Frog and Toad have different tastes in clothing. Imagine and describe how each one might dress. Why?

16 Why do you think the author chose not to give Frog and Toad other names?

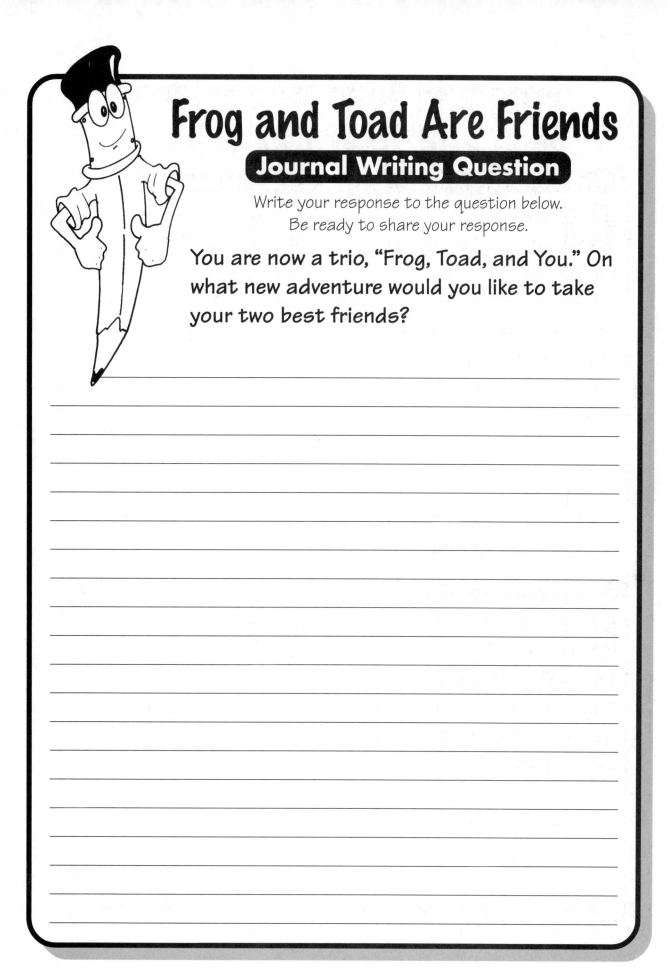

Frog and Toad Are Friends

Journal Writing Question

Write your response to the question below.
Be ready to share your response.

You are now a trio, "Frog, Toad, and You." On what new adventure would you like to take your two best friends?

_____
_____
_____
_____
_____
_____
_____
_____
_____
_____
_____
_____
_____
_____
_____
_____
_____

Frog and Toad Are Friends
Question Starters

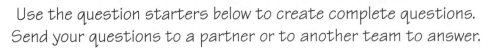

Use the question starters below to create complete questions.
Send your questions to a partner or to another team to answer.

1. Would you rather _____

_____

2. What might Frog _____

_____

3. If you were Toad _____

_____

4. What would have happened if _____

_____

5. What was your favorite _____

_____

6. Where might Frog and Toad _____

_____

7. What does this story _____

_____

8. Will Frog and Toad _____

_____

Higher-Level Thinking Questions for Primary Literature
Kagan Publishing • 1 (800) 933-2667 • www.KaganOnline.com

Goldilocks and the Three Bears

higher-level thinking questions

"Most people would sooner die than think; in fact, they do so.

— Bertrand Russell"

Higher-Level Thinking Questions for Primary Literature
Kagan Publishing • 1 (800) 933-2667 • www.KaganOnline.com

Goldilocks and the Three Bears
Question Cards

Goldilocks and the Three Bears

1 Retell the story from the point of view of Baby Bear.

Goldilocks and the Three Bears

2 How are you like Goldilocks?

Goldilocks and the Three Bears

3 How would the story be different if Goldilocks had found the gingerbread house in "Hansel and Gretel" instead of the three bears' house?

Goldilocks and the Three Bears

4 How could Father Bear have acted differently? Create a new story with a different Father Bear.

Goldilocks and the Three Bears
Question Cards

Goldilocks and the Three Bears

5 Would you have gone inside the bears' home if you were Goldilocks? Why or why not?

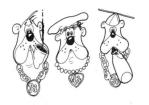

Goldilocks and the Three Bears

6 Think of one word to describe Goldilocks.

Goldilocks and the Three Bears

7 Create a new adventure for Goldilocks.

Goldilocks and the Three Bears

8 Suppose Goldilocks is on trial for "trespassing" and you are the judge. Will you find her guilty and punish her? Explain your decision.

Higher-Level Thinking Questions for Primary Literature
Kagan Publishing • 1 (800) 933-2667 • www.KaganOnline.com

Goldilocks and the Three Bears
Question Cards

Goldilocks and the Three Bears

9 What could happen if Goldilocks did not get away?

Goldilocks and the Three Bears

10 Does Goldilock's bad day remind you of a day in your life? How?

Goldilocks and the Three Bears

11 Suppose the three bears did not go out for a walk, but instead laid down for a nap. Make the story turn out differently.

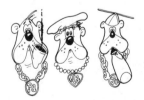

Goldilocks and the Three Bears

12 Would you like to have Goldilocks as a good friend?

Goldilocks and the Three Bears
Question Cards

Goldilocks and the Three Bears

13 If you were Goldilocks, what would you have told your mother when you got home?

Goldilocks and the Three Bears

14 Compare Goldilock's experiences with Jack's in "Jack and the Beanstalk."

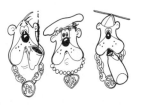

Goldilocks and the Three Bears

15 What other accidents might have occurred if the three bears hadn't returned so soon?

Goldilocks and the Three Bears

16 What might Goldilocks do for the three bears to show that she is sorry?

Higher-Level Thinking Questions for Primary Literature
Kagan Publishing • 1 (800) 933-2667 • www.KaganOnline.com

Goldilocks...
Journal Writing Question

Write your response to the question below.
Be ready to share your response.

Create a new adventure for Goldilocks.

_____

_____

_____

_____

_____

_____

_____

_____

_____

_____

_____

_____

_____

_____

_____

_____

_____

Goldilocks...

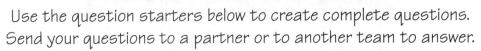
Question Starters

Use the question starters below to create complete questions.
Send your questions to a partner or to another team to answer.

1. Do you think Goldilocks _____

_____

2. If you were one of the bears _____

_____

3. What part _____

_____

4. What would have happened if _____

_____

5. Would you ever _____

_____

6. What is the difference between _____

_____

 7. If the story _____

_____

8. Could Goldilocks _____

_____

Higher-Level Thinking Questions for Primary Literature
Kagan Publishing • 1 (800) 933-2667 • www.KaganOnline.com

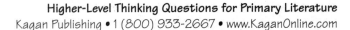

Hansel and Gretel

higher-level thinking questions

"

In teaching it is the method and not the content that is the message...the drawing out, not the pumping in.

"

— Ashley Montague

Higher-Level Thinking Questions for Primary Literature
Kagan Publishing • 1 (800) 933-2667 • www.KaganOnline.com

Hansel and Gretel
Question Cards

Hansel and Gretel

1 How might Hansel find his home in some other way?

Hansel and Gretel

2 Decide which parts of the story could happen today.

Hansel and Gretel

3 What might have happened if no one lived in the gingerbread house?

Hansel and Gretel

4 Were Hansel and Gretel's parents "good" parents? Why or why not?

Hansel and Gretel

5 How would you feel if you found the gingerbread house? What would you do?

Hansel and Gretel

6 Compare Gretel to Goldilocks. How are they alike and different?

Hansel and Gretel

7 Pretend the three bears found the gingerbread house when Hansel and Gretel were inside. How might the story turn out?

Hansel and Gretel

8 Were Hansel and Gretel brave? Explain your answer.

Higher-Level Thinking Questions for Primary Literature
Kagan Publishing • 1 (800) 933-2667 • www.KaganOnline.com

Hansel and Gretel
Question Cards

Hansel and Gretel

9 How might you have been different if you were Gretel in the story?

Hansel and Gretel

10 Who in the story is like someone you know? How?

Hansel and Gretel

11 Pretend the witch was a good witch. How might the story change?

Hansel and Gretel

12 Which character would you like to be? Why?

Hansel and Gretel

13 Retell the story from the witch's point of view.

Hansel and Gretel

14 What do you think the witch was thinking as Hansel and Gretel approached her house?

Hansel and Gretel

15 Create a new adventure for Hansel and Gretel.

Hansel and Gretel

16 What do you think Hansel and Gretel learned from this experience?

Higher-Level Thinking Questions for Primary Literature
Kagan Publishing • 1 (800) 933-2667 • www.KaganOnline.com

Hansel and Gretel

Journal Writing Question

Write your response to the question below.
Be ready to share your response.

Retell the story from the witch's point of view.

_____

_____

_____

_____

_____

_____

_____

_____

_____

_____

_____

_____

_____

_____

_____

_____

_____

_____

_____

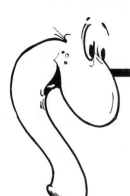

Hansel and Gretel
Question Starters

Use the question starters below to create complete questions.
Send your questions to a partner or to another team to answer.

1. How would you feel if

2. If you were the witch

3. What is your favorite

4. If the story was

5. Why did the author

6. How could you explain

7. Do you agree

8. What similarities

Higher-Level Thinking Questions for Primary Literature
Kagan Publishing • 1 (800) 933-2667 • www.KaganOnline.com

Jack and the Beanstalk

higher-level thinking questions

"Learning without thought is useless. Thought without learning is dangerous.

— Confucius

Higher-Level Thinking Questions for Primary Literature
Kagan Publishing • 1 (800) 933-2667 • www.KaganOnline.com

Jack and the Beanstalk
Question Cards

Jack and the Beanstalk

1 Describe the new and different things Jack saw when he got to the top of the beanstalk.

Jack and the Beanstalk

2 Name three reasons Jack was afraid of the giant.

Jack and the Beanstalk

3 Suppose Jack did not meet the man with the magic seeds. Instead he traded the cow for a bicycle. Explain what might have happened.

Jack and the Beanstalk

4 What did Jack and his mother do with the giant?

Jack and the Beanstalk
Question Cards

Jack and the Beanstalk

5 Jack's mother sent Jack to town to sell the cow. How could Jack and his mother have kept the cow and started a business with it?

Jack and the Beanstalk

6 What feelings was Jack having when he first reached the top of the beanstalk?

Jack and the Beanstalk

7 Did Jack have the right to take things from the giant's house?

Jack and the Beanstalk

8 Was Jack right in chopping down the beanstalk as the giant was climbing down? Why or why not?

Higher-Level Thinking Questions for Primary Literature
Kagan Publishing • 1 (800) 933-2667 • www.KaganOnline.com

Jack and the Beanstalk
Question Cards

Jack and the Beanstalk

9 Decide whether Jack was a "good" or "bad" son. Why?

Jack and the Beanstalk

10 If you woke up and saw a giant beanstalk outside your window, would you climb it? Explain your answer.

Jack and the Beanstalk

11 Suppose you were in the giant's house... Would you stay long? Where would you sleep or hide?

Jack and the Beanstalk

12 Was the giant a mean giant? Explain, and give evidence from the story.

Jack and the Beanstalk
Question Cards

Jack and the Beanstalk

13 At the end of the story, was the giant dead or just knocked out? Then, what happened?

Jack and the Beanstalk

14 Retell the story making the giant a kind person.

Jack and the Beanstalk

15 If your mother sent you to sell the cow and you met the man with the magic beans, what would he need to say to you to trade your cow for his beans?

Jack and the Beanstalk

16 How might the story change if Jack were Jackie (a girl)?

Higher-Level Thinking Questions for Primary Literature
Kagan Publishing • 1 (800) 933-2667 • www.KaganOnline.com

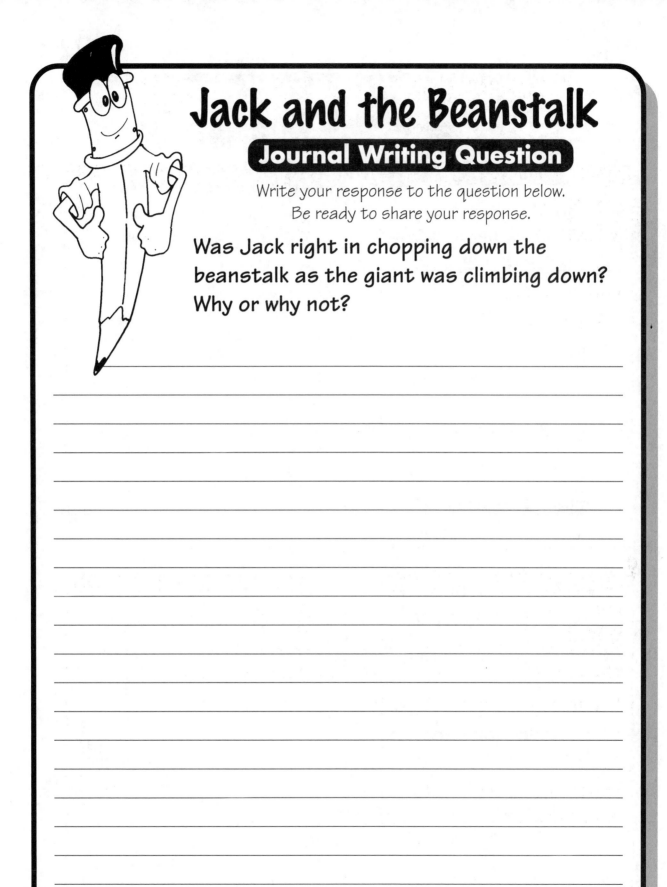

Jack and the Beanstalk

Journal Writing Question

Write your response to the question below.
Be ready to share your response.

Was Jack right in chopping down the beanstalk as the giant was climbing down? Why or why not?

Jack and the Beanstalk
Question Starters

Use the question starters below to create complete questions.
Send your questions to a partner or to another team to answer.

1. If you were the giant

2. What could Jack

3. How might the story

4. Compare this story

5. In your own life

6. What could you say about

7. How would you evaluate

8. How did the characters

Higher-Level Thinking Questions for Primary Literature
Kagan Publishing • 1 (800) 933-2667 • www.KaganOnline.com

The Little
Mermaid

higher-level thinking questions

"Imagination is more important than knowledge.

— Albert Einstein

Higher-Level Thinking Questions for Primary Literature
Kagan Publishing • 1 (800) 933-2667 • www.KaganOnline.com

The Little Mermaid
Question Cards

The Little Mermaid

1 Retell the story from Prince Eric's point of view?

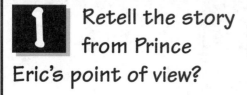

The Little Mermaid

2 What do you think Ariel was thinking when Ursula disguised herself as a maiden and used Ariel's voice?

The Little Mermaid

3 Suppose Triton lost his magical powers and in the end could not grant Ariel her wish. What might happen next?

The Little Mermaid

4 Was Triton a good father? What parts of the story show this?

The Little Mermaid
Question Cards

The Little Mermaid

5 If you were Ariel, how would you feel if your father destroyed your treasures?

The Little Mermaid

6 Compare Cinderella's stepmother to Ursula.

The Little Mermaid

7 Imagine Prince Eric found out Ariel was a mermaid. How might the story be different?

The Little Mermaid

8 Will Ariel be a good wife for Prince Eric? Why or why not?

Higher-Level Thinking Questions for Primary Literature
Kagan Publishing • 1 (800) 933-2667 • www.KaganOnline.com

The Little Mermaid
Question Cards

9 How would you have helped Ariel when she had no voice? In real life who would you like to help?

10 How are you like or unlike Ariel?

11 Invent several ways Ariel could have disguised the fact that she was a mermaid.

12 Which character was most clever? Why?

The Little Mermaid

13 Retell the story from the point of view of Sebastian the crab.

The Little Mermaid

14 Identify the parts of the story that show how Ariel felt about Prince Eric.

The Little Mermaid

15 Pretend Ariel never met Prince Eric. Create a new ending for the story.

The Little Mermaid

16 Choose the character you would most like to meet. Why?

Higher-Level Thinking Questions for Primary Literature
Kagan Publishing • 1 (800) 933-2667 • www.KaganOnline.com

The Little Mermaid
Journal Writing Question

Write your response to the question below.
Be ready to share your response.

Pretend Ariel never met Prince Eric. Create a new ending for the story.

_____
_____
_____
_____
_____
_____
_____
_____
_____
_____
_____
_____
_____
_____
_____
_____
_____
_____
_____
_____

The Little Mermaid
Question Starters

Use the question starters below to create complete questions.
Send your questions to a partner or to another team to answer.

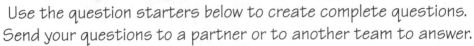

1. How might Ariel _____

_____

2. Compare Ursula _____

_____

3. What did Triton _____

_____

4. How would you feel _____

_____

5. If the story was _____

_____

6. If you were the author _____

_____

7. How would you describe _____

_____

8. What conclusions can you make _____

_____

Higher-Level Thinking Questions for Primary Literature
Kagan Publishing • 1 (800) 933-2667 • www.KaganOnline.com

Little Red Riding Hood

higher-level thinking questions

"The human mind is our fundamental resource.

— John F. Kennedy "

Higher-Level Thinking Questions for Primary Literature
Kagan Publishing • 1 (800) 933-2667 • www.KaganOnline.com

Little Red Riding Hood
Question Cards

Little Red Riding Hood

1 When Little Red Riding Hood was in trouble she yelled for help. What else might she have done?

Little Red Riding Hood

2 When Little Red Riding Hood got to the woods she met the wolf. How would the story change if she had met a crow?

Little Red Riding Hood

3 Will Little Red Riding Hood's mother send her through the forest again to visit Grandma? What should she tell her before she leaves home?

Little Red Riding Hood

4 Red is the color of danger. List things that are red for this reason.

Little Red Riding Hood
Question Cards

Little Red Riding Hood

5 Why do you think authors have wolves play the bad roles in stories? What other animals might play that role?

Little Red Riding Hood

6 The setting has changed so that Grandma's house is an apartment complex in a large city. Instead of meeting a wolf she meets _____.
How does the story change?

Little Red Riding Hood

7 Have your grandparents or parents ever given you something very special that you liked as much as Little Red Riding Hood loved her coat? Tell about it.

Little Red Riding Hood

8 How is Little Red Riding Hood like and unlike you?

Higher-Level Thinking Questions for Primary Literature
Kagan Publishing • 1 (800) 933-2667 • www.KaganOnline.com

Little Red Riding Hood
Question Cards

Little Red Riding Hood

9 Compare the characters Goldilocks and Little Red Riding Hood. (Similarities and differences)

Little Red Riding Hood

10 Do you know any other stories that have a wolf as a main character? How are they alike and different from this one?

Little Red Riding Hood

11 What might have happened if the woodcutter did not show up?

Little Red Riding Hood

12 If Little Red Riding Hood were your daughter and you could change one thing about her, what would it be?

Little Red Riding Hood
Question Cards

Little Red Riding Hood

13 Did the woodcutter have the right to shoot the wolf? Why or why not?

Little Red Riding Hood

14 The wolf answered, "Big ears are better to hear you with." "Big eyes are better to see you with." Is bigger always better? Explain your answer.

Little Red Riding Hood

15 Have you ever done something you were told not to do and got into trouble? Explain.

Little Red Riding Hood

16 Which character in the story would you like to be? Why?

Higher-Level Thinking Questions for Primary Literature
Kagan Publishing • 1 (800) 933-2667 • www.KaganOnline.com

Little Red Riding Hood

Journal Writing Question

Write your response to the question below.
Be ready to share your response.

Did the woodcutter have the right to shoot the wolf? Why or why not?

_____

_____

_____

_____

_____

_____

_____

_____

_____

_____

_____

_____

_____

_____

_____

_____

_____

_____

Little Red Riding Hood
Question Starters

Use the question starters below to create complete questions.
Send your questions to a partner or to another team to answer.

1. What do you think the wolf

2. How would you describe

3. What might happen if

4. Where do you think

5. If you were Little Red Riding Hood

6. What is the difference between

7. Would you ever

8. What do you predict

Higher-Level Thinking Questions for Primary Literature
Kagan Publishing • 1 (800) 933-2667 • www.KaganOnline.com

Pinocchio

higher-level thinking questions

"

The most important educational goal is learning to learn.

—Dr. Luis Alberto Machado, Creating the Future

"

Higher-Level Thinking Questions for Primary Literature
Kagan Publishing • 1 (800) 933-2667 • www.KaganOnline.com

Pinocchio
Question Cards

Pinocchio

1 If you were dubbed "Pinocchio's Official Conscience," how would you have advised him?

Pinocchio

2 Describe the relationship between Pinocchio and Jiminy Cricket.

Pinocchio

3 In what other ways could Pinocchio have proven he was brave, truthful, and unselfish?

Pinocchio

4 What do you think Pinocchio learned from his experiences?

Pinocchio
Question Cards

Pinocchio

5 How might Pinocchio have saved himself from Foulfellow the Fox?

Pinocchio

6 How did Pinocchio feel about Pleasure Island?

Pinocchio

7 If the story continued, what else might happen?

Pinocchio

8 What do you think might have happened if Jiminy Cricket were not in the story?

Higher-Level Thinking Questions for Primary Literature
Kagan Publishing • 1 (800) 933-2667 • www.KaganOnline.com

Pinocchio
Question Cards

Pinocchio

9 What did Pinocchio learn from this experience?

Pinocchio

10 The Blue Fairy made Pinocchio prove himself before making him a real boy. How is this like real life?

Pinocchio

11 Retell the story from the Blue Fairy's point of view.

Pinocchio

12 What kind of real boy will Pinocchio be? Explain your answer.

Pinocchio

13 Have you ever found yourself guided to do things you shouldn't? Explain.

Pinocchio

14 Why did Foulfellow the Fox keep selling Pinocchio?

Pinocchio

15 Imagine what might have happened if Pinocchio had remained a wooden boy.

Pinocchio

16 Pinocchio went into the sea to save his father from the whale. What were all the risks? What could he gain?

Higher-Level Thinking Questions for Primary Literature
Kagan Publishing • 1 (800) 933-2667 • www.KaganOnline.com

Pinocchio

Journal Writing Question

Write your response to the question below.
Be ready to share your response.

If the story continued, what else might happen?

_____

_____

_____

_____

_____

_____

_____

_____

_____

_____

_____

_____

_____

_____

_____

_____

_____

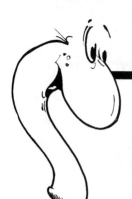

Pinocchio

Question Starters

Use the question starters below to create complete questions.
Send your questions to a partner or to another team to answer.

1. What might have happened if
_____
_____

2. Why was Pinocchio
_____
_____

3. What is your favorite
_____
_____

4. What part of the story
_____
_____

5. Who does Jiminy Cricket
_____
_____

6. What effects
_____
_____

7. How do you relate
_____

8. What changes
_____
_____

Higher-Level Thinking Questions for Primary Literature
Kagan Publishing • 1 (800) 933-2667 • www.KaganOnline.com

Rumplestiltskin

higher-level thinking questions

Spoon feeding in the long run teaches us nothing but the shape of the spoon.

— E. M. Forster

Higher-Level Thinking Questions for Primary Literature
Kagan Publishing • 1 (800) 933-2667 • www.KaganOnline.com

Rumplestiltskin
Question Cards

Rumplestiltskin

1 What would you have told Rumpelstiltskin if you were the girl?

Rumplestiltskin

2 Are you more like Rumpelstiltskin or the girl?

Rumplestiltskin

3 What happened to Rumpelstiltskin? Pretend he was alive today. What might he do?

Rumplestiltskin

4 Was Rumpelstiltskin "good" or "bad"? Why?

Rumplestiltskin
Question Cards

5 If you had magical powers, who would you help? Why?

6 Compare Rumpelstiltskin to a character in another story. Who does he seem most like?

7 Think of other ways the girl could have been saved.

8 Did the girl make a good decision by promising Rumpelstiltskin her first child? Explain.

Higher-Level Thinking Questions for Primary Literature
Kagan Publishing • 1 (800) 933-2667 • www.KaganOnline.com

Rumplestiltskin
Question Cards

Rumplestiltskin

9 Retell the story from Rumpelstiltskin's point of view.

Rumplestiltskin

10 Do you think the girl and her father were close?

Rumplestiltskin

11 What else might Rumpelstiltskin have asked for besides the firstborn child?

Rumplestiltskin

12 What could the girl's father have done differently?

Rumplestiltskin
Question Cards

Rumplestiltskin

13 Would you have wanted to marry the king? Why or why not?

Rumplestiltskin

14 Was there ever a time when you couldn't do something that someone thought you could? Explain your answer.

Rumplestiltskin

15 Imagine Rumpelstiltskin never showed up in the first place. What do you think the king would have done with the girl?

Rumplestiltskin

16 Can you think of a situation when a promise should not be kept? Justify your answer.

Higher-Level Thinking Questions for Primary Literature
Kagan Publishing • 1 (800) 933-2667 • www.KaganOnline.com

Rumplestiltskin

Journal Writing Question

Write your response to the question below.
Be ready to share your response.

Was Rumpelstiltskin "good" or "bad"? Why?

Rumplestiltskin

Question Starters

Use the question starters below to create complete questions.
Send your questions to a partner or to another team to answer.

1. What would motivate

2. Is the story better

3. How would you feel

4. How is Rumplestiltskin different

5. What effect did the setting

6. What would you do if

7. How would you describe

8. Where might

Higher-Level Thinking Questions for Primary Literature
Kagan Publishing • 1 (800) 933-2667 • www.KaganOnline.com

Sleeping Beauty

higher-level thinking questions

"Untilled soil, however fertile it may be, will bear thistles and thorns; and so it is with a man's mind.

— Teresa of Avila

Sleeping Beauty
Question Cards

Sleeping Beauty

1 If you had the power to give two special gifts, what would you give? Who would you give them to?

Sleeping Beauty

2 Compare Sleeping Beauty with Snow White. How are they alike and different?

Sleeping Beauty

3 You have been invited to the party as a good fairy. What gift would you give the newborn princess?

Sleeping Beauty

4 Did the author select a good title for the story? Can you make a better title?

Sleeping Beauty
Question Cards

Sleeping Beauty

5 Which three questions would you like to ask the prince when you awoke from a long sleep.

Sleeping Beauty

6 How might the story be different if Sleeping Beauty were the only one to fall asleep?

Sleeping Beauty

7 Pretend Sleeping Beauty didn't want to marry the prince. Create a new ending for the story.

Sleeping Beauty

8 What kind of queen do you think Sleeping Beauty will make? Explain your answer.

Higher-Level Thinking Questions for Primary Literature
Kagan Publishing • 1 (800) 933-2667 • www.KaganOnline.com

Sleeping Beauty
Question Cards

Sleeping Beauty

9 If you had a fairy godmother that could grant you three wishes, what would they be?

Sleeping Beauty

10 What caused Sleeping Beauty to prick her finger?

Sleeping Beauty

11 How would the story be different if the king and queen had a son instead of a daughter?

Sleeping Beauty

12 Is Sleeping Beauty anything like you? Why or why not?

Sleeping Beauty
Question Cards

Sleeping Beauty

13 If this curse were placed on you, which person in your life would be most upset? What might they do?

Sleeping Beauty

14 Which parts of the story could not happen in real life?

Sleeping Beauty

15 Suppose the queen had told Sleeping Beauty about the evil curse placed on her. How might the story have changed?

Sleeping Beauty

16 What would have happened if Sleeping Beauty had never found the spinning wheel?

Higher-Level Thinking Questions for Primary Literature
Kagan Publishing • 1 (800) 933-2667 • www.KaganOnline.com

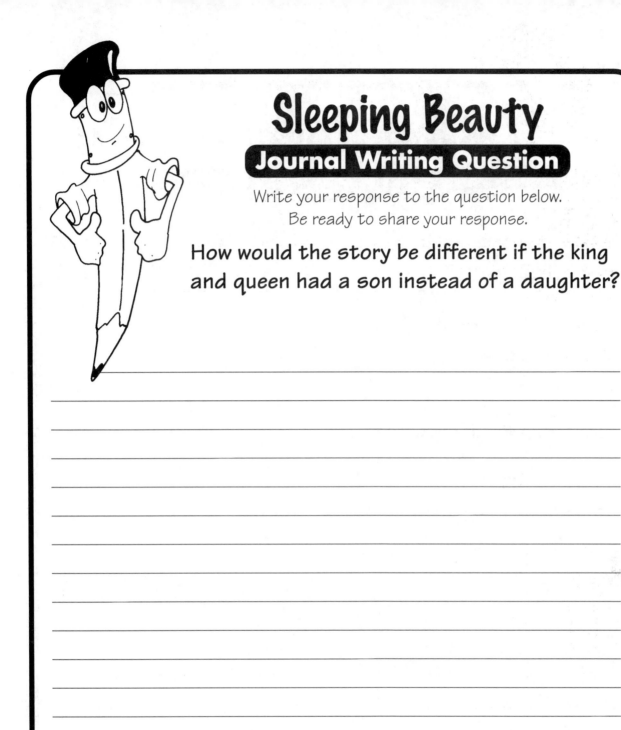

Sleeping Beauty

Journal Writing Question

Write your response to the question below.
Be ready to share your response.

How would the story be different if the king and queen had a son instead of a daughter?

_____

_____

_____

_____

_____

_____

_____

_____

_____

_____

_____

_____

_____

_____

_____

_____

_____

_____

_____

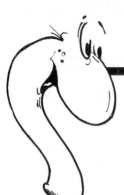

Sleeping Beauty
Question Starters

Use the question starters below to create complete questions.
Send your questions to a partner or to another team to answer.

1. Which character

2. What does this story

3. How would you describe the relationship

4. What would be different if

5. Do you prefer

6. If you were Sleeping Beauty

7. At which point

8. In your own life

Higher-Level Thinking Questions for Primary Literature
Kagan Publishing • 1 (800) 933-2667 • www.KaganOnline.com

Snow White

higher-level thinking questions

"The true aim of everyone who aspires to be a teacher should be, not to impart his own opinions, but to kindle minds.

— Frederick William Robertson

Higher-Level Thinking Questions for Primary Literature
Kagan Publishing • 1 (800) 933-2667 • www.KaganOnline.com

Snow White
Question Cards

Snow White

1 Think of another story character with an evil character. How is that story like this one?

Snow White

2 In what ways is Snow White like Goldilocks?

Snow White

3 Suppose Snow White were not beautiful. How might the story be different?

Snow White

4 Which dwarf is your favorite? Why?

Snow White
Question Cards

Snow White

5 What would you have done if the huntsman left you deep in the forest?

Snow White

6 Compare Snow White's life to Cinderella's.

Snow White

7 Imagine Snow White running into her stepmother years later. What might they say to each other?

Snow White

8 Would Snow White make a good friend? Why or why not?

Higher-Level Thinking Questions for Primary Literature
Kagan Publishing • 1 (800) 933-2667 • www.KaganOnline.com

Snow White
Question Cards

Snow White

9 Pretend you are Snow White talking with the seven dwarfs. What would you say to them?

Snow White

10 Have you ever been lost? Compare your experience with Snow White's.

Snow White

11 Think of other ways Snow White could have been saved if the seven dwarfs weren't around.

Snow White

12 Was Snow White treated fairly by her stepmother? What parts of the story support your opinion?

Higher-Level Thinking Questions for Primary Literature
Kagan Publishing • 1 (800) 933-2667 • www.KaganOnline.com

Snow White
Question Cards

Snow White

13 How is Snow White like or unlike Sleeping Beauty?

Snow White

14 How would the story change if Snow White had never met the seven dwarfs?

Snow White

15 Did Snow White's stepmother do a good job disguising herself?

Snow White

16 What is the moral of the story?

Higher-Level Thinking Questions for Primary Literature
Kagan Publishing • 1 (800) 933-2667 • www.KaganOnline.com

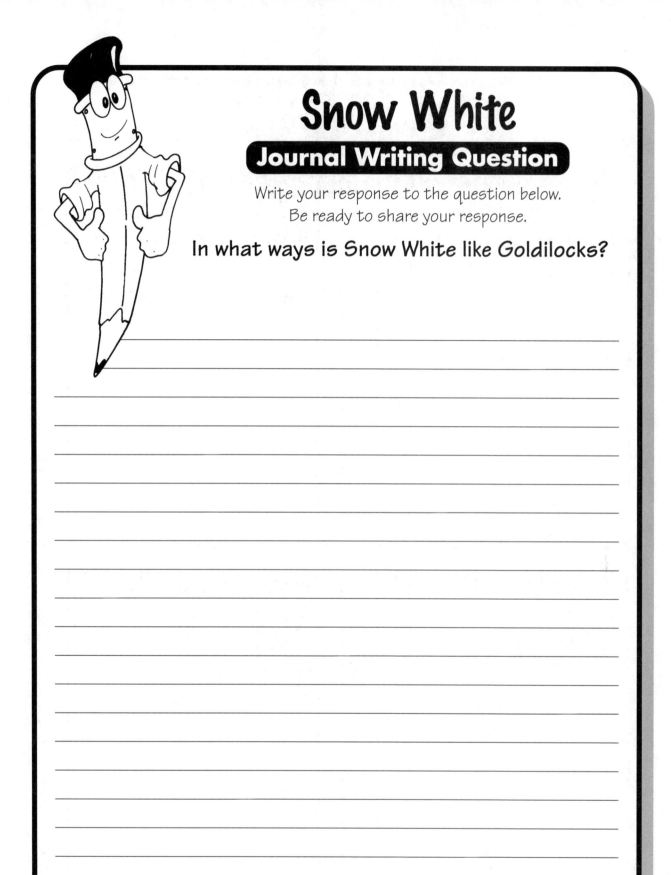

Snow White

Journal Writing Question

Write your response to the question below.
Be ready to share your response.

In what ways is Snow White like Goldilocks?

Snow White

Question Starters

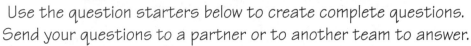

Use the question starters below to create complete questions.
Send your questions to a partner or to another team to answer.

1. What was the cause of

2. Why do you think

3. If you were Snow White

4. If the dwarfs

5. If you could

6. How would you describe

7. What would happen if

8. How is this story different

Higher-Level Thinking Questions for Primary Literature
Kagan Publishing • 1 (800) 933-2667 • www.KaganOnline.com

Stone Soup

higher-level thinking questions

"You cannot teach people anything. You can only help them discover it within themselves."

— Galileo

Higher-Level Thinking Questions for Primary Literature
Kagan Publishing • 1 (800) 933-2667 • www.KaganOnline.com

Stone Soup
Question Cards

Stone Soup

1 If food were scarce, where would you hide food in your house? Why would you choose that place?

Stone Soup

2 Who are you more like, the soldiers or the villagers? Why?

Stone Soup

3 How would the story have been different if the villagers brought out only salt and pepper?

Stone Soup

4 Do you think the soldiers had really entertained the king? Why or why not?

Stone Soup
Question Cards

Stone Soup

5 What would you have done if you were the soldier and were refused food and a place to sleep?

Stone Soup

6 Could the story really happen? What is the story like in real life?

Stone Soup

7 Make up a new title for the story.

Stone Soup

8 Did the villagers ever find out they had been tricked? What might they do if they had found out?

Higher-Level Thinking Questions for Primary Literature
Kagan Publishing • 1 (800) 933-2667 • www.KaganOnline.com

Stone Soup
Question Cards

Stone Soup

9 Suppose you lived in the village. Would you have given the soldiers food?

Stone Soup

10 How are the soldiers like or unlike you?

Stone Soup

11 Create a new ending to the story in which the soldiers settled down in the village.

Stone Soup

12 If you were choosing a friend, would it be a soldier or a villager? Why?

Stone Soup
Question Cards

Stone Soup

13 What did the soldiers learn from this experience? What did the villagers learn?

Stone Soup

14 How would you describe the villagers' feelings about the soldiers?

Stone Soup

15 In what other ways could the soldiers have gotten food?

Stone Soup

16 Did the villagers deserve what happened? What could they learn from what happened?

Higher-Level Thinking Questions for Primary Literature
Kagan Publishing • 1 (800) 933-2667 • www.KaganOnline.com

Stone Soup

Journal Writing Question

Write your response to the question below.
Be ready to share your response.

Create a new ending to the story in which the soldiers settled down in the village.

_____
_____
_____
_____
_____
_____
_____
_____
_____
_____
_____
_____
_____
_____
_____
_____
_____
_____

Stone Soup

Question Starters

Use the question starters below to create complete questions.
Send your questions to a partner or to another team to answer.

1. Would you prefer _____

_____

2. Why might _____

_____

3. How could the story _____

_____

4. If you were a character _____

_____

5. What part of the story _____

_____

6. How would you describe the relationship _____

_____

7. What conclusions can you draw _____

_____

8. What similarities _____

_____

Higher-Level Thinking Questions for Primary Literature
Kagan Publishing • 1 (800) 933-2667 • www.KaganOnline.com

Teacher From the Black Lagoon

"I've known countless people who were reservoirs of learning yet never had a thought."

— Wilson Mizner

Higher-Level Thinking Questions for Primary Literature
Kagan Publishing • 1 (800) 933-2667 • www.KaganOnline.com

 # Teacher From the Black Lagoon
Question Cards

Teacher From the Black Lagoon

1 Pretend the teacher from the Black Lagoon is a mom. What does she probably do at home?

Teacher From the Black Lagoon

2 If the teacher from the Black Lagoon were like a fairy godmother, how might the story change?

Teacher From the Black Lagoon

3 How is the teacher from the Black Lagoon like or unlike your teacher?

Teacher From the Black Lagoon

4 You have been voted by the class to get rid of the teacher from the Black Lagoon. How would you go about it?

Teacher From the Black Lagoon

5 Did the illustrator draw the characters well? Why or why not?

Teacher From the Black Lagoon

6 Why do you think the teacher from the Black Lagoon acted the way she did?

Teacher From the Black Lagoon

7 When the boy awakes from his dream, the teacher from the Black Lagoon is really there — create a new ending.

Teacher From the Black Lagoon

8 Try to make up a better title for the story.

Higher-Level Thinking Questions for Primary Literature
Kagan Publishing • 1 (800) 933-2667 • www.KaganOnline.com

Teacher From the Black Lagoon
Question Cards

9 Make up a sequel to the story: "The Student from the Black Lagoon."

10 Rank the tragedies in the story from bad to very bad.

11 You are the boy's best friend. Design a plan to sneak him out of the classroom.

12 What was your favorite part of the story? Why?

Teacher From the Black Lagoon
Question Cards

Teacher From the Black Lagoon

13 You are a news reporter writing an article about the teacher from the Black Lagoon. What is the headline of your article?

Teacher From the Black Lagoon

14 What was the principal thinking when he stuck his head in the door? How do we know this?

Teacher From the Black Lagoon

15 Pretend you were a student in the classroom. What would you do?

Teacher From the Black Lagoon

16 Which student in the classroom is most like you? In what way?

Higher-Level Thinking Questions for Primary Literature
Kagan Publishing • 1 (800) 933-2667 • www.KaganOnline.com

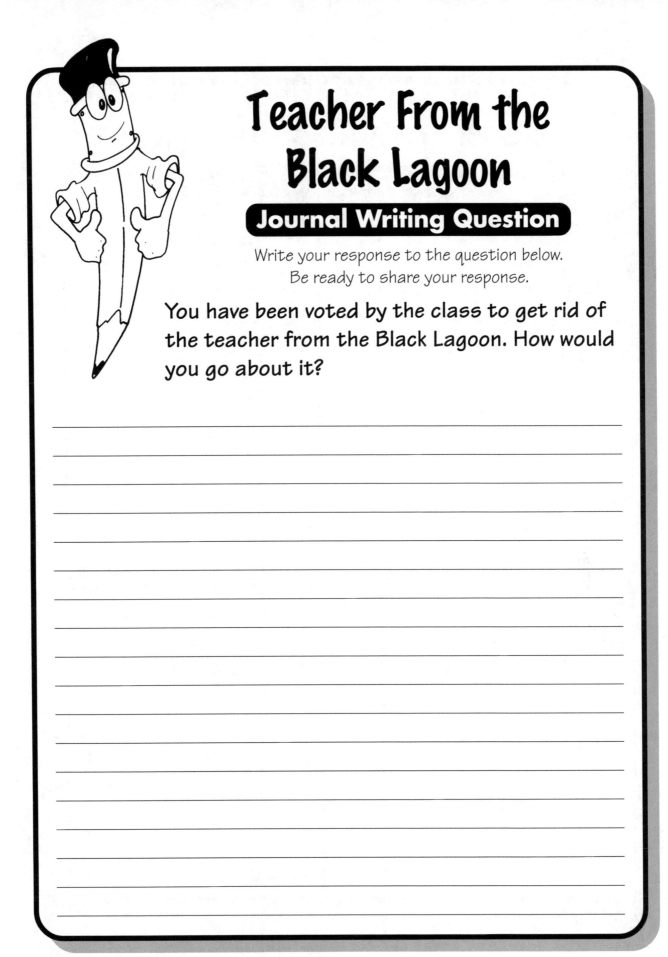

Teacher From the Black Lagoon

Journal Writing Question

Write your response to the question below.
Be ready to share your response.

You have been voted by the class to get rid of the teacher from the Black Lagoon. How would you go about it?

Teacher from the Black Lagoon
Question Starters

Use the question starters below to create complete questions.
Send your questions to a partner or to another team to answer.

1. How do you feel when

_____

_____

2. Why might

_____

_____

3. In your own experience

_____

_____

4. Have you ever

_____

_____

5. What might the Black Lagoon

_____

_____

6. Is daydreaming

_____

_____

7. Who would

_____

8. What would be worse

_____

Higher-Level Thinking Questions for Primary Literature
Kagan Publishing • 1 (800) 933-2667 • www.KaganOnline.com

The Three Little Pigs

higher-level thinking questions

> # Learning is not just knowing the answers.
>
> — Charles Handy,
> The Age of Unreason

Higher-Level Thinking Questions for Primary Literature
Kagan Publishing • 1 (800) 933-2667 • www.KaganOnline.com

Three Little Pigs
Question Cards

Three Little Pigs

1 How would you describe the personality of a pig that chooses to build his home out of straw rather than bricks?

Three Little Pigs

2 If the main character were a man instead of a wolf, how might the story change?

Three Little Pigs

3 Retell the story starting with the wolf on the roof of the brick house and the three pigs inside.

Three Little Pigs

4 If you were going to make your "home out of bricks," what would you do differently?

Three Little Pigs
Question Cards

Three Little Pigs

5 The three pigs build each of their houses out of different materials. What are some good and bad features of each material?

Three Little Pigs

6 Make up a new ending for the story.

Three Little Pigs

7 Make up a story in which the pigs used their money in a way other than buying building materials.

Three Little Pigs

8 Name three possible characteristics of students who'd choose to "build their house out of straw." (Example: they don't do their homework.)

Higher-Level Thinking Questions for Primary Literature
Kagan Publishing • 1 (800) 933-2667 • www.KaganOnline.com

Three Little Pigs
Question Cards

Three Little Pigs

9 Which of the three pigs is most like you and why?

Three Little Pigs

10 What could you do to make the wolf never want to come by your house?

Three Little Pigs

11 The three pigs go to the clothing store where each picks out different clothing. Describe what each might be wearing and tell why.

Three Little Pigs

12 Would you rather be a pig or the wolf in the story? Why?

Three Little Pigs
Question Cards

Three Little Pigs

13 Who is the "wolf" in your life?

Three Little Pigs

14 Your straw house just got blown down by the wolf. Would you hide in the straw, fight back, or run? Tell why.

Three Little Pigs

15 Could three pigs live happily ever after in the brick house? What problems might they have?

Three Little Pigs

16 If you were the wolf, how would you get the three pigs out of the brick house? Describe your plan.

Three Little Pigs

Journal Writing Question

Write your response to the question below.
Be ready to share your response.

If you were the wolf, how would you get the three pigs out of the brick house? Describe your plan.

Three Little Pigs
Question Starters

Use the question starters below to create complete questions.
Send your questions to a partner or to another team to answer.

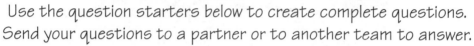

1. Which little pig

2. If you were the wolf

3. What would have happened if

4. What relationship

5. How did the story

6. What can you conclude

7. Do you agree

8. What do you think

Higher-Level Thinking Questions for Primary Literature
Kagan Publishing • 1 (800) 933-2667 • www.KaganOnline.com

Notes